BABY BIRDS

hatch out of their eggs and face the world in different ways. Some chicks are able to run and feed themselves right away. Others are blind and naked at hatching and need to be fed by their parents. Some chicks spend almost no time at their nest, while others can be there for up to two months. Birds nest in a variety of ways, from on the ground to high up in the trees. Some nests are out in the open. Others are carefully hidden in trees or bushes. Most baby birds, as well as their parents, are camouflaged so that predators can't find them easily.

In this book you will meet all kinds of baby birds and their families. So the next time you are out for a walk, you might recognize a familiar face!

BLACK TERN

Baby Birds
in the Wild

PHOTOGRAPHS BY D

For Riley

Heritage House Publishing Company Ltd.
heritagehouse.ca

Cataloguing information available from Library and Archives Canada

978-1-77203-064-8 (pbk)

Cover and book design by Jacqui Thomas
Cover and title page photos by Damon Calderwood: Rufous hummingbird (*front cover*);
pygmy nuthatch (*title page*); vesper sparrow (*back cover*).

This book was produced using FSC-certified, acid-free paper, processed
chlorine free, and printed with soya-based inks.

Heritage House acknowledges the financial support for its publishing program from the
Government of Canada through the Canada Book Fund (CBF) and the Canada Council
for the Arts, and the Province of British Columbia through the British Columbia Arts
Council and the Book Publishing Tax Credit.

19 18 17 16 15 1 2 3 4 5

Printed in China

BARN OWL

RED-WINGED BLACKBIRD

BLACK-NECKED STILT

WILLOW FLYCATCHER

SPOTTED SANDPIPER

AMERICAN ROBIN

ALDER FLYCATCHER

BREWER'S SPARROW

AMERICAN AVOCET

SNOWY PLOVER

ANNA'S HUMMINGBIRD

COOPER'S HAWK

BLACK-HEADED GROSBEAK

LAZULI BUNTING

CEDAR WAXWING

LOGGERHEAD SHRIKE

NORTHERN MOCKINGBIRD

COMMON REDPOLL

MARSH WREN

COMMON YELLOWTHROAT

NORTHERN CARDINAL

CRISSAL THRASHER

WESTERN KINGBIRD

DUSKY FLYCATCHER

WHITE CROWNED SPARROW

MOUNTAIN BLUEBIRD

VIRGINIA RAIL

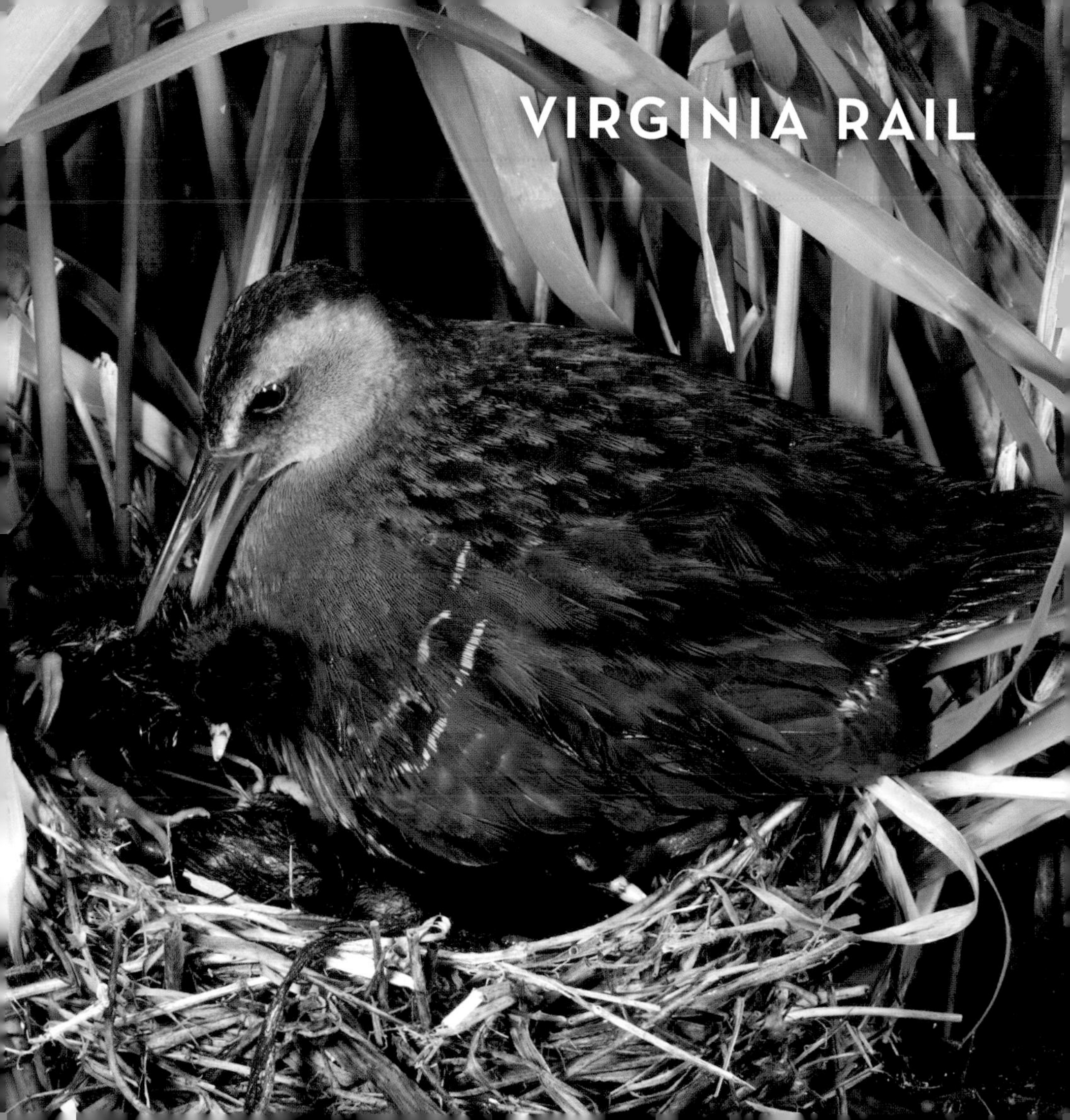

AMERICAN GOLDFINCH

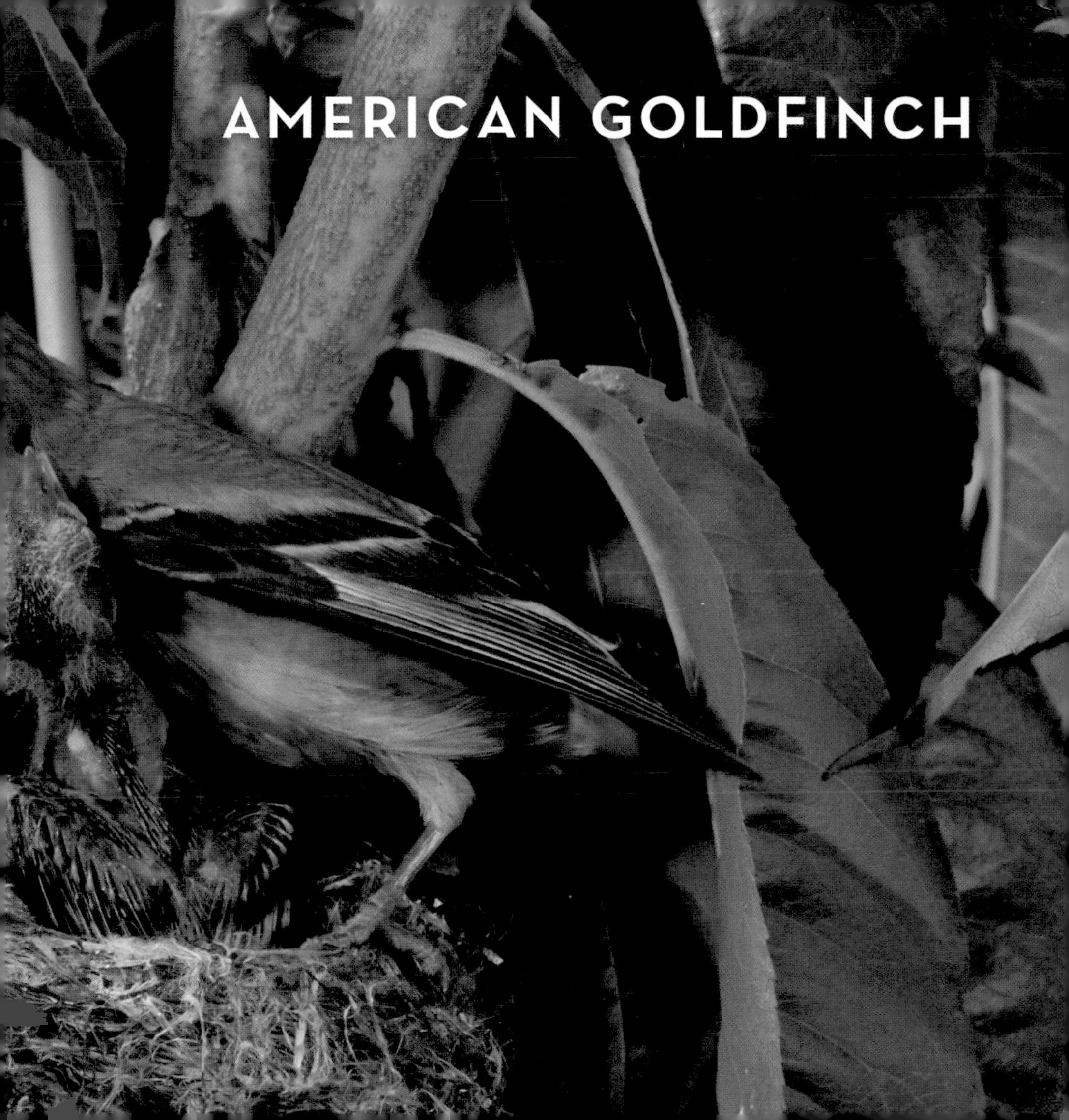

NORTHERN FLICKER

ORANGE-CROWNED WARBLER

NORTHWESTERN CROW

RUFOUS HUMMINGBIRD

PLUMBEOUS VIREO

SAGE THRASHER

WILLETT

WESTERN SCRUB-JAY

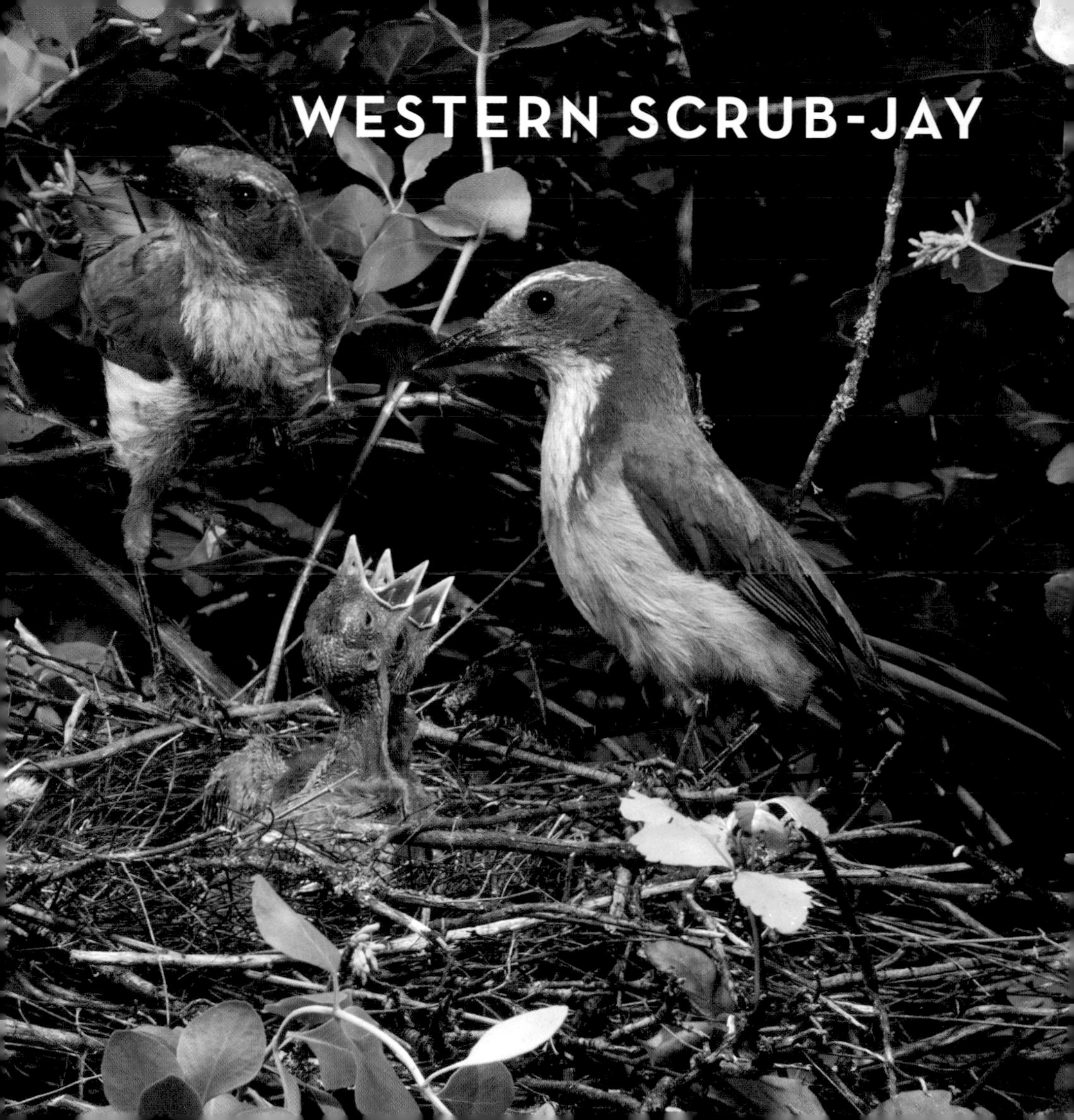

VERDIN

SEMIPALMATED PLOVER

VESPER SPARROW

SWAINSON'S THRUSH

WESTERN SCREECH-OWL